Popular Italian Madrigals of the
Sixteenth Century

Popular Italian Madrigals of the Sixteenth Century for Mixed Voices

Edited by Alec Harman

Oxford University Press
Music Department, 37 Dover Street, London W1X 4AH

ISBN 0 19 343646 9

Foreword

It is a truism that the popularity of a work of art is sometimes ephemeral, often local, and nearly always subject to fluctuations. Since the eighteenth century, when concerts first became a common feature of the musical scene, the popularity of a particular composition has been gauged by the frequency of its public performances, but in earlier centuries the only reliable guide to the popularity of a piece was the number of times it was copied or printed.

In preparing this collection of 'popular' sixteenth-century Italian madrigals I restricted myself to what are, in my opinion, the principal composers of this genre, namely: Festa, Verdelot, Arcadelt, Willaert, Rore, Palestrina, Lassus, A. Gabrieli, Monte, Wert, Marenzio, Gesualdo, and Monteverdi. I added a further restriction of only selecting those works by the above composers that were included in at least four sixteenth- or early seventeenth-century prints that were substantially different from each other. In other words, I have discounted the number of times a particular madrigal book was reprinted – unless the contents of a reprint are markedly different from an earlier edition – because the reprinting of a whole book only indicated the book's popularity, not that of an individual madrigal. Thus, concerning Willaert's *Amor mi fa morire*, for example, I have counted separately Verdelot's second book of madrigals *a*4 (1536) – which first contained this particular piece – and the reprint of the first and second books combined (1544), because the second book in the 1544 print contains only 16 madrigals out of 30 that are identical with the 23 in the 1536 edition. Similarly with other editions that seem from the title to be the same. On the other hand, concerning Rore's *Ancor che col partire*, I have counted his first book of madrigals *a*4 (1550), in which this piece appears, but have not counted Gardano's edition (1577) of all of Rore's four-voiced madrigals, because it contains all the madrigals previously published in the first and second books.

There is one exception to the above-mentioned restrictions, namely, I have added Domenico Ferrabosco to the list of composers, because his *Io mi son giovinetta* was included in more widely differing publications than any other madrigal.

The purpose of this collection is two-fold. First, to add a fairly representative selection of Italian madrigals to the lamentably few that are available in modern, modestly-priced editions suitable for use by both amateurs and professionals, and in the university classroom. Second, to list the seventeen madrigals which can, I think, reasonably be claimed to be the majority, if not all, of the most popular Italian madrigals of the period, and to provide the opportunity for observing just how popular a particular madrigal was and over what span of years. For such an observation I append the sources for each madrigal, the latter being arranged chronologically according to its first occurrence in print. I have also included the name of the author (where known), the essential references in VogelV, RISM, and EinB, and brief comments where necessary or desirable, including quotations from and/or references to EinIM and BroIMP.

Unfortunately it has not been possible, for economic reasons, to include all seventeen madrigals in this edition, and so for those composers who wrote two or more popular madrigals I have selected only one. Of the resulting ten madrigals in this collection four are based on 'complete' editions (some are still in progress); the remainder I have transcribed from microfilms of the earliest intact sixteenth-century print, with one exception. The precise source I have used is asterisked.

I have indicated at the beginning of each piece the original clefs, signatures, note-values, and pitches, and have footnoted black notes (but not ligatures) and errors. Most of the transcriptions are transposed in order to make, with very few exceptions, the highest notes of the soprano and tenor parts g'' and g' respectively, and the lowest note of the alto part g; in only two cases is the transcription more than a whole tone up or down. Additional accidentals which I believe to be necessary are printed small. Changes in time-signature not in the original are enclosed in square brackets, as are other editorial additions, unless footnoted, except, of course, the barring.

The tempo indication which I have added at the beginning of each piece is intended to be approximate, but it always implies two minim beats per bar, the one exception being Wert's *D'un si bel foco*, for rhythmic reasons which I think are obvious. I have not indicated dynamics or expression marks as these should be dictated by the sense of the words and the musical importance of a particular voice in relation to the other voices.

The Italian texts have been modernised (the sources for the poems by Petrarch and Boccaccio are given in the comments on the relevant madrigals), and the English translations follow the rhyme scheme and metre of the originals, and also attempt to match exactly the position of those words and phrases that evoke a descriptive musical figure or passage. Such translations present considerable difficulties, and while for the literal meaning of the texts I have been assisted by and am extremely grateful to Professor Antonio Pace of the University of Washington and, more especially, my daughter Anna, I am responsible for any obscurity or awkwardness in the end result.

I wish to express my thanks to those librarians of the libraries given below who provided me with microfilms of the following madrigal books:

Accademia filarmonica, Verona – Arcadelt: first book *a*3, 1542.

Bayerische Staatsbibliothek, Munich – Wert: first book *a*4, 1561. *Musica di XIII autori*, 1576.

Biblioteca del Conservatorio, Bologna – Verdelot: second book *a*4, 1536.

Delli madrigali a tre, 1537. *Madrigali a tre*, 1559. A. Gabrieli: second book *a*6, 1580. Marenzio: fifth book *a*6, 1591.

British Museum, London – *Musica divina*, 1583.

Herzog-August-Bibliothek, Wolfenbüttel – *Madrigali a tre*, 1537.

Staats- und Stadtbibliothek, Augsburg – Wert: first book *a4*, 1564.

Finally, this collection, entailing as it has the listing of literally thousands of madrigal titles, would have been impossible without Emil Vogel's outstanding piece of research, and Alfred Einstein's revision of it. To both these scholars I, along with many others, owe an enormous debt.

University of Washington, 1973   ALEC HARMAN

Reference Abbreviations

BroIMP   Brown, H.M. *Instrumental Music Printed Before 1600.* 1965.

EinB   'Bibliography of Italian Secular Vocal Music Printed Between the Years 1500–1700. By Emil Vogel. Revised and enlarged by Alfred Einstein.' *Notes II* (1945), 185,275; III (1945), 51, (1946), 154, 256, 363; IV (1946), 41, (1947), 201, 301; V (1947), 65, (1948), 277, 385, 537.

EinIM   Einstein, A. *The Italian Madrigal.* 3 vols. 1949.

RISM   *Répertoire International des Sources Musicales.* I,1. 1960.

VogelV   Vogel, E. *Bibliothek der Gedruckten Weltlichen Vocalmusik Italiens. Aus den Jahren ·1500-1700.* 2 vols. 1892.

Sources

I Willaert   Amor mi fa morire (B. Dragonetto) (Thou, Love, dost cause my dying)

1. *Il secondo libro de madrigali di Verdelot* . . . . Scotto, 1536. (VogelV: Verdelot No. 8; RISM: 1536⁷).

2. *Verdelot a quatro voci* . . . . Gardano, 1544. (VogelV: Verdelot No. 8d; RISM: 1544¹⁸).

3. *Madrigali a quatro voci* . . . . Scotto, 1563. (VogelV: Willaert No. 5).

4. *Musicale essercitio di Ludovico Balbi* . . . . Gardano, 1589. (VogelV: 1589⁴; RISM: 1589¹²).

In source No. 4 only the top voice is Willaert's; the lower three have been added by Balbi.

Arcadelt   Ingiustissimo Amor, perchè sì raro (Ariosto: *Orlando furioso*, II,1) (O iniquitous Love, wherefore so rarely)

1. *Delli madrigali a tre voci. B* Scotto, 1537. (VogelV: 1537³; RISM: 1537⁷).

2. *Madrigali a tre et arie napolitane* . . . . [1537?]. (VogelV: [1537²]; RISM: [c.1537]⁸).

3. *Primo libro di madrigali d'Archadelt a tre voci* . . . . Gardano, 1542. (VogelV: Arcadelt No. 41; RISM: 1542¹³).

4. *Madrigali a tre voci* . . . . Scotto, 1559. (VogelV: 1559³; RISM: 1559²⁰).

In sources Nos. 1, 2, and 4, all of which are incomplete, this particular madrigal is anonymous, but the surviving parts are identical with those of Arcadelt's setting in source No. 3.

II Arcadelt   Il bianco e dolce cigno (Alfonso d'Avalos) (The white and gentle swan)

1. *Il primo libro di madrigali . . . a quatro* . . . . Gardano, 1539. (VogelV: Arcadelt No. 1; RISM: 1539²²).

2. *Dialogo della musica di M. Antonfrancesco Doni* . . . . Scotto, 1544. (VogelV: 1544¹; RISM: 1544²²).

3. *Il primo libro di madrigali a quatro voci* . . . . Rampazzetto, 1566. (VogelV: Arcadelt No. 15; RISM: 1566²⁵).

4. *Musicale essercitio di Ludovico Balbi.* . . . . Gardano, 1589. (VogelV: 1589⁴; RISM: 1589¹²).

5. *Madrigalia quattro. . . . coretto. . . . da Claudio Monteverde* . . .

Masotti, 1627. (VogelV: Arcadelt No. 27; RISM: 1627⁷).
It is possible that the first edition (1538?) is lost. EinIM
says that this madrigal was 'reprinted again and again',
being 'the most famous piece of Arcadelt's entire madrigal
production' (I, 269), and that it was the 'most widely
diffused and most famous madrigal of the time' (I, 186),
but he is confusing the book (which went through nearly
forty editions between the first and last in 1654) with the
madrigal itself. In sources Nos. 2 and 4 only the top voice
is Arcadelt's; the lower 3 have been added by Doni and
Balbi respectively. The author is given as G. Guidiccioni
in EinB (1544¹ and 1589⁴), but EinIM states that 'the text
sometimes ascribed to Giovanni Guidiccioni. . . .is actually
by Alfonso d'Avalos' (I, 269). BroIMP gives two arrangements (1554, 1562).

III Ferrabosco   Io mi son giovinetta, e volentieri (Boccaccio: *Decameron* —
   (Domenico)   end of ninth day) (O young am I, and gladly without
                     ceasing)
   1. *Il primo libro d'i madrigali de diversi. . . . autori. . . .quatuor*
   vocum. . . . Gardano, 1542.
   (VogelV: 1542²; RISM: 1542¹⁷).
   2. *Il primo libro d'i madrigali de diversi autori. . . a quatro*
   voci. . . . Gardano, 1546. (VogelV: 1546¹; RISM: 1546¹⁵).
   3. *Il secondo libro de madrigali de diversi autori. . . . a quatro*
   voci. . . . Scotto, 1567. (VogelV: 1567³; RISM: 1567¹⁵).
   4. *La eletta di tutta la musica intitolata corona. . . . libro*
   primo. . . [Zorzi?], 1569. (VogelV: 1569³ᵃ; RISM: 1569²⁰).
   5. *Livre de meslanges contenant un recueil de chansons a quatre*
   parties. . . . Phalèse & Bellère, 1575. (VogelV: 1575³;
   RISM: 1575⁴).
   6. **Musica divina de XIX. autori illustri. . . .* Phalèse &
   Bellère, 1583. (VogelV: 1583²; RISM: 1583¹⁵).
   7. *Gemma musicalis;. . . . .liber primus. . . .* Gerlach, 1588.
   (VogelV: 1588²; RISM: 1588²¹).
   8. *Nuova spoglia amorosa. . . .* Vincenti, 1593. (VogelV:
   1593⁴; RISM: 1593⁵).
   9. *Di Camillo Lambardi. . . .Il primo libro di madrigali à*
   quattro voci. . . . Carlino, 1600. (VogelV: C. Lambardi No.
   1; RISM: 1600¹³).
   10. *Arcadelt il primo libro de' madrigali à quattro voci. . . .*
   Sottile, 1608. (VogelV: Arcadelt No. 23a; RISM: 1608¹¹).
   EinIM (I, 308) says that the 'effect' of this madrigal
   'almost surpassed Arcadelt's *Il bianco e dolce cigno*', My
   source for the text is the *Opere di Giovanni Boccaccio* (ed.

Segre): *I Classici Italiani*, Vol. III. BroIMP gives 13 arrangements between 1563 and 1596.

Willaert

Qual più diversa e nova cosa fu mai (What object more diverse and strange was there e'er)

1. *Madrigali a quatro voce di Geronimo Scotto.* . . . Scotto, 1542. (VogelV: Scotto No. 1; RISM: 1542[19]).

2. *Il vero terzo libro di madrigali de diversi autori.* . . . Gardano, 1549. (VogelV: 1549[2]; RISM: 1549[31]).

3. *Madrigali a quatro voci di Adriano Willaert.* . . . Scotto, 1563. (VogelV: Willaert No. 5).

4. *La eletta di tutta la musica intitolata corona.* . . . [Zorzi?] 1569. (VogelV: 1569[3a]; RISM: 1569[20]).

IV Rore

Ancor che col partire (Alfonso d'Avalos) (Though when from thee I'm parting)

1. *Primo libro di madrigali a quatro voci di Perissone.* . . . Gardano, 1547. (VogelV: Perissone No. 3; RISM: 1547[14]).

2. *Madrigali de la fama a quattro voce.* . . . Scotto, 1548. (VogelV: 1548[1]; RISM: 1548[8]).

3. *Il primo libro de madrigali a quatro voci.* . . .Bugehat, 1550. (VogelV: Rore No. 36).

4. *La eletta di tutta la musica intitolata corona.* . . . [Zorzi?], 1569. (VogelV: 1569[3a]; RISM: 1569[20]).

5. *Musica divina di XIX. autori illustri.* . . . Phalèse & Bellère, 1583. (VogelV: 1583[2]; RISM: 1583[15]).

6. *Gemma musicalis.* . . . Gerlach, 1588. (VogelV: 1588[2]; RISM: 1588[21]).

7. *Musicale essercitio di Ludovico Balbi.* . . . Gardano, 1589. (VogelV: 1589[4]; RISM: 1589[12]).

8. *Nuova spoglia amorosa.* . . . Vincenti, 1593. (VogelV: 1593[4]; RISM: 1593[5]).

9. *Archadet il primo libro de' madrigali à quattro voci.* . . . Sottile, 1608. (VogelV: Arcadelt No. 23a; RISM: 1608[14]).

10. *Opera Omnia*, IV (ed. Meier): *Corpus Mensurabilis Musicae*, 14.

EinIM (I, 403-4) says that this was 'the most famous of all' Rore's madrigals, and that 'there were dozens of arrangements, paraphrases, and parodies for the lute and other instruments': he also claims 'that there can be no doubt that the poem contributed also to its unparalleled success'. (Cf. also I, 374; II, 525, 796.) In source No. 7 only the top voice is Rore's; the lower 3 have been added by Balbi. In EinB the author is incorrectly given as Guidiccioni in one print (1569[3a]); elsewhere, and in EinIM (I, 404), it is given as Alfonso d'Avalos. BroIMP gives

20 arrangements between 1560 and 1596.

Lassus Per pianto la mia carne si distilla (Sannazaro) (Through weeping my poor flesh, alas, distilleth)
1. *Il primo libro dove si contengono madrigali, villanesche.* . . . Susato, 1555. (VogelV: Lassus No. 50; RISM: 1555[29]).
2. *Il primo libro delli madrigali. . . a quattro voci.* . . . Dorico, 1560. (VogelV: Lassus No. 39; RISM: 1560[18]).
3. *Harmonia celeste.* . . . Phalèse & Bellère, 1583. (VogelV: 1583[1]; RISM: 1583[14]).
4. *Musicale essercitio di Ludovico Balbi.* . . . Gardano, 1589. (VogelV: 1589[4]; RISM: 1589[12]).
In source No. 4 only the top voice is by Lassus; the lower 3 have been added by Balbi. BroIMP gives 5 arrangements between 1568 and 1594.

Wert Cara la vita mia (Dear one, my life's sweet darling)
1. *Il primo libro de madrigali a cinque voci.* . . . Scotto, 1558. (Vogel: Wert No. 1).
2. *Musica divina di XIX. autori illustri.* . . . Phalèse & Bellère, 1583. (VogelV: 1583[2]; RISM: 1583[15]).
3. *Spoglia amorosa* . . . . Scotto, 1584. (EinB: 1584[1a]; RISM: 1584[5]).
4. *Scielta de madrigali a' cinque voci. . . accommodati in motetti.* . . . Tini & Lomazzo, 1604. (VogelV: 1604[3]; RISM: 1604[11]).
5. *Nervi d'Orfeo.* . . . de' Haestens, 1605. (VogelV: 1605[2]; RISM: 1605[9]).
BroIMP gives 2 arrangements (1584, 1599).

Wert Chi salirà per me (Ariosto: *Orlando furioso*, XXXV, 1) (Who, lady, will ascend)
1. *Secondo libro delle muse, a quattro voci.* . . . Barré, 1558. (VogelV: 1558[1]; RISM: 1558[13]).
2. *Il primo libro de madrigali a quatro voci.* . . . Gardano, 1564. (VogelV: Wert No. 31).
3. *Symphonia angelica.* . . . Phalèse & Bellère, 1585. (VogelV: 1585[1]; RISM: 1585[19]).
4. *Musica transalpina.* . . . Yonge, 1588. (VogelV: 1588[1]; RISM: 1588[29]).
5. *Musicale essercitio di Ludovico Balbi.* . . . Gardano, 1589. (VogelV: 1589[4]; RISM: 1589[12]).
6. *Nuova spoglia amorosa.* . . . Vincenti, 1593. (VogelV: 1593[4]; RISM: 1593[5]).
VogelV states that the contents of the first edition (1561) of Wert's first book *a4* (Wert No. 29) are the same as the 1564 edition, save for the fourth from last madrigal; in fact

the last four madrigals, including *Chi salirà*, are missing from the 1561 edition. EinIM says that Wert 'won especial fame' with this madrigal (II, 517). In source No. 5 only the top voice is Wert's; the lower 3 have been added by Balbi. BroIMP gives one arrangement (1584).

Lassus

Appariran per me le stelle in cielo (They will appear for me, the stars in heaven)

1. *Il primo libro delli madrigali. . . .a quattro voci. . . .* Dorico, 1560. (VogelV: Lassus No. 39; RISM: 1560[18]).
2. *Livre de meslanges contenant un recueil de chansons a quatre parties. . . .* Phalèse & Bellère, 1575. (VogelV: 1575[3]; RISM: 1575[4]).
3. *Harmonia celeste. . . .* Phalèse & Bellère, 1583. (VogelV: 1583[1]; RISM: 1583[14]).
4. *Nuova spoglia amorosa. . . .* Vincenti, 1593. (VogelV: 1593[4]; RISM: 1593[5]).

BroIMP gives 4 arranegments between 1568 and 1584.

Palestrina

Io son ferito, ahi lasso (Wounded am I, ah sadly)

1. *Il terzo libro delle muse a cinque voci. . . .* Gardano, 1651. (VogelV: 1561[3]; RISM: 1561[10]).
2. *Prima stella. De madrigali a cinque voci . . . .* Scotto, 1570. (VogelV: 1570[2]; RISM: 1570[16]).
3. *Gemma musicalis . . . .* Gerlach, 1588. (VogelV: 1588[2]; RISM: 1588[21]).
4. *Nuova spoglia amorosa. . . .* Vincenti, 1593. (VogelV: 1593[4]; RISM: 1593[5]).
5. *Paradiso musicale de madrigale et canzoni a cinque voci. . . .* Phalèse, 1596. (VogelV: 1596[3]; RISM: 1596[10]).

EinIM says that this madrigal left 'a deep impression upon [Palestrina's] contemporaries' (I, 318), and that it was parodied by Marenzio (third book of villanelle – 1585), Hassler (1590), and Vecchi (1597) among others (II, 590-92), and quoted by Marenzio (fifth book of madrigals a5 – 1585) and Vecchi (1587) (II, 643 and 780 respectively. Cf. also I, 212). BroIMP gives 5 arrangements between 1568 and 1594.

V Palestrina

Vestiva i colli/Così le chiome mie (H. Capilupi) (Clothed the hills/Thus sweetly speaking)

1. *Il desiderio secondo libro di madrigali a cinque voci. . . .* Scotto, 1566. (VogelV: 1566[3]; RISM: 1566[3]).
2. *Musica divina de XIX. autori illustri. . . .* Phalèse & Bellère, 1583. (VogelV: 1583[2]; RISM: 1583[15]).
3. *Spoglia amorosa. . . .* Scotto, 1584. (EinB: 1584[1a]; RISM: 1584[5]).

4. *Musica transalpina.* . . . Yonge, 1588. (VogelV: 1588[1]; RISM: 1588[29]).

5. *Gemma musicale* . . . . Gerlach, 1588. (VogelV: 1588[2]; RISM: 1588[21]).

6. *Spoglia amorosa.* . . . Gardano, 1592. (VogelV: 1592[6]; RISM 1592[15]).

7. *Nuova spoglia amorosa.* . . . Vincenti, 1593. (VogelV: 1593[4]; RISM: 1593[5]).

8. **Le Opere Complete*, IX (ed. Casimiri).

EinIM says that this madrigal left 'a deep impression upon [Palestrina's] contemporaries' (I, 318), and that it was parodied by Vecchi (1587) and Banchieri (1598) (II, 780 and 804 respectively), and quoted by Belli (1584) (I, 212. Cf. also II, 842). BroIMP gives 9 arrangements between 1568 and 1596.

VI Monte   Ahi, chi mi rompe il sonno/Di ch'ella mossa (D. Veniero) (Ah, who disturbs my slumbers/Said she with ardour)

1. *Il terzo libro delli madrigali, à cinque voci.* . . . Scotto, 1570. (VogelV: Monte No. 31).

2. *Musica divina di XIX autori illustri.* . . . Phalèse & Bellère, 1583. (VogelV: 1583[2]; RISM: 1583[15]).

3. *Spoglia amorosa.* . . . Scotto, 1584. (EinB: 1584[1a]; RISM: 1584[5]).

4. *Spoglia amorosa.* . . . Gardano, 1592. (VogelV: 1592[6]; RISM: 1592[15]).

5. **Opera Omnia.* XXV (ed. Van den Borren).

An incomplete copy of *Nuova scelta di madrigali di sette autori.* . . . Carlino, 1615 (VogelV: 1615[1]; RISM: 1615[14]) contains an anonymous madrigal on this text, which may be Monte's. BroIMP gives one arrangement (1593).

VII Wert   D'un sì bel foco/Scorgo tanto alto il lume (With such fair flames/See I on high the light)

1. **Musica di XIII. autori illustri a cinque voci.* . . . Gardano, 1576. (VogelV: 1576[1]; RISM: 1576[5]).

2. *Harmonia celeste.* . . . Phalèse & Bellère, 1583. (VogelV: 1583[1]; RISM: 1583[14]).

3. *Gemma musicalis.* . . . Gerlach, 1588. (VogelV: 1588[2]; RISM 1588[21]).

4. *Scielta de madrigali a' cinque voci. . . accommodati in motetti.* . . . Tini & Lomazzo, 1604. (VovelV: 1604[3]; RISM: 1604[11]).

BroIMP gives 2 arrangements (1584, 1593).

VIII Lassus   S'io esca vivo (Petrarch: Rime LXXX, verse 6 to end)

(If 'scape I living)

1. *Corona de madrigali a sei voci.* . . . Scotto, 1579. (VogelV: 1579[1]; RISM: 1579[2]).

2. *Harmonia celeste.* . . . Phalèse & Bellère, 1583. (VogelV: 1583[1]; RISM: 1579[14]).

3. *Gemma musicalis.* . . . Gerlach, 1588. (VogelV: 1588[2]; RISM: 1588[21]).

4. *La fleur des chansons d'Orlande de Lassus.* . . . Phalèse & Bellère, 1592. (VogelV: Lassus No. 59; RISM 1592[9]).

5. *Nervi d'Orfeo.* . . . de' Haestens, 1605. (VogelV: 1605[2]; RISM: 1605[9]).

6. **Sämtliche Werke*, X (ed. Haberl and Sandberger).

My source for the text is *Rime, Trionfi e Poesie Latine* (ed. Neri, Martellotti, Bianchi, Sapegna).

IX Gabrieli
(Andrea)

Sonno diletto e caro (Sleep, thou beloved treasure)

1. **Il secondo libro de madrigali a sei voci.* . . . Gardano, 1580. (VogelV: A. Gabrieli No. 4).

2. *Symphonia angelica.* . . . Phalèse & Bellère, 1585. (VogelV: 1585[1]; RISM: 1585[19]).

3. *Musica tolta da i madrigali di Claudio Monteverde* . . . . Tradate, 1607. (VogelV: Monteverdi No. 54; RISM: 1607[20]).

4. *Fatiche spirituali di Simone Molinaro.* . . . Amadino, 1610. (VogelV: 1610[3]; RISM: 1610[2]).

X Marenzio

Leggiadre ninfe (L. Guicciardi) (Ye graceful nymphs)

1. **Il quinto libro de madrigali a sei voci.* . . . Gardano, 1591. (VogelV: Marenzio No. 16; RISM: 1591[21]).

2. *Il trionfi di Dori.* . . . Gardano, 1592. (VogelV: 1592[2]; RISM: 1592[11]).

3. *Nervi d'Orfeo.* . . . de' Haestens, 1605. (VogelV: 1605[2]; RISM: 1605[9]).

4. *Fatiche spirituali di Simone Molinaro.* . . . Amadino, 1610. (VogelV: 1610[3]; RISM: 1610[2]).

5. *Erster Theil lieblicher, welscher Madrigalien.* . . . Halbmayer, 1624. (VogelV/EinB: 1624[1]; RISM: 1624[16]).

This madrigal may also be in *Lucae Marentii.* . . . *madrigalia sex vocum.* . . . Kauffmann, 1608 (VogelV: Marenzio No.24). EinIM says that the piece was commissioned by the Venetian patrician Leonardo Sanudo for a wedding (II, 667). BroIMP gives one arrangement (1599).

Contents

POPULAR ITALIAN MADRIGALS
of the
SIXTEENTH CENTURY
Edited by Alec Harman
1. AMOR MI FA MORIRE

Adrian Willaert
(*c.* 1480–1562)

Printed in Great Britain

OXFORD UNIVERSITY PRESS, MUSIC DEPARTMENT, 37 DOVER STREET, LONDON W1X 4AH

*) ♩ (= ♪)

4

* **Black semibreve and minim.**

2. IL BIANCO E DOLCE CIGNO

Jakob Arcadelt
(*c.* 1514–*c.* 1567)

*) Black semibreve and minim.

3. IO MI SON GIOVINETTA, E VOLENTIERI

Domenico Maria Ferrabosco
(1513–1574)

16

-re, mer-zé d'a - mo-re e de' dol - ci_____ pen - sie - ri.
-pid, all thanks to love and to thoughts sweet - ly_____ pleas - ing.

- mor, mer-zé d'a - mo-re e de' dol - ci pen - sie - ri.
love, all thanks to love and to thoughts sweet - ly pleas - ing.

- mor, mer-zé d'a - mo-re e de' dol - ci pen - - - sie - ri.
love, all thanks to love and to thoughts sweetly_____ pleas - ing.

- mor, mer-zé d'a - mor e de' dol - ci pen-sie - ri.
love, all thanks to love and to thoughts sweetly pleas - ing.

22 [Pt. 2]

Io_____ vo_____ pe' ver - di pra - ti,
Lo_____ through_____ the gras-sy mead - ows,

Io vo pe' ver - di pra - ti, io vo pe' ver - di
Lo through the gras-sy mead - ows, lo through the gras-sy

Io vo_____ pe' ver - di
Lo through_____ the gras-sy

Io vo pe'
Lo through the

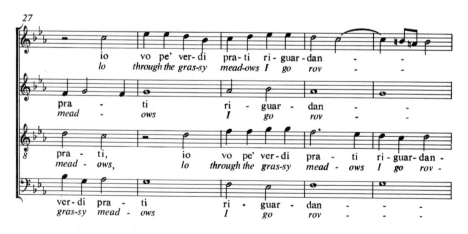

27

io vo pe' ver - di pra - ti ri - guar-dan - -
lo through the gras-sy mead-ows I go rov - -

pra - ti ri - guar - dan - -
mead - ows I go rov - -

pra - ti, io vo pe' ver - di pra - ti ri - guar-dan -
mead - ows, lo through the gras-sy mead - ows I go rov -

ver - di pra - ti ri - guar - dan - - -
gras-sy mead - ows I go rov - - -

4. ANCOR CHE COL PARTIRE

Cipriano de Rore
(1516–1565)

18

*)Repeat written out in full in original.

5. VESTIVA I COLLI

Giovanni Pierluigi da Palestrina
(*c.* 1525–1594)

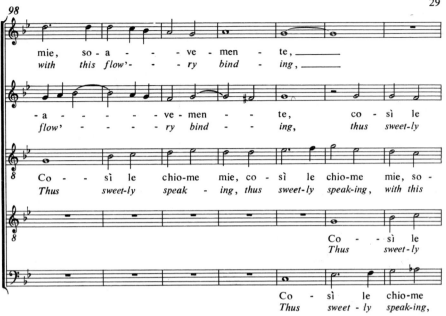

98

mie, so - a - - - ve - men - te, _____
with this flow'- - - ry bind - ing, _____

- a - - - - - ve - men - - te, co - sì le
flow' - - - - ry bind - - ing, thus sweet-ly

Co - sì le chio-me mie, co - sì le chio-me mie, so -
Thus sweet-ly speak - ing, thus sweet-ly speak-ing, with this

Co - sì le
Thus sweet-ly

Co - sì le chio-me
Thus sweet - ly speak-ing,

105

so - a - ve - men - - - - - - - te _____
this flow'-ry bind - - - - - - - ing _____

chio-me mie, so - a - ve - men - - te Par -
speak-ing, with this flow'-ry bind - - ing My

- a - ve - men- te, so - a - ve - men - te
flow'-ry bind-ing, this flow' - ry bind - ing

chio - me mie, so - a - ve - men - te _____
speak-ing, with this flow'- ry bind - ing _____

mie, so - a - ve - men - - te Par - lan - do jo
with this flow'ry bind - - ing My hair I

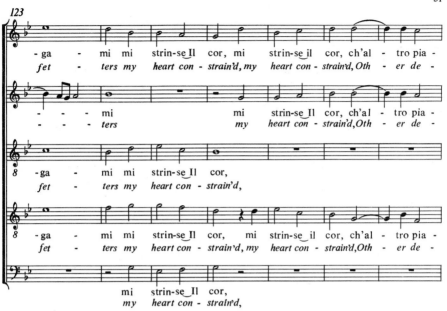

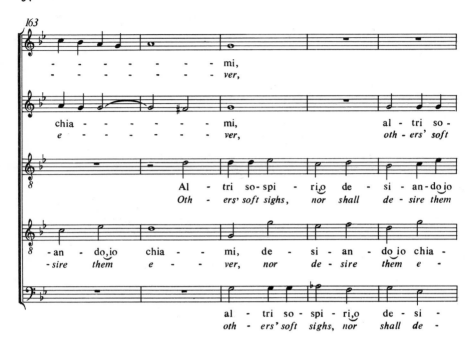

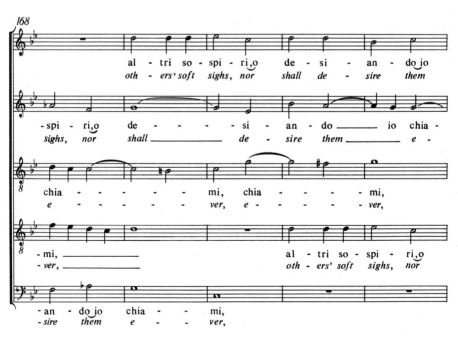

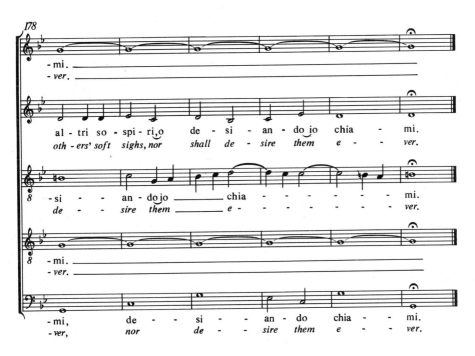

6. AHI, CHI MI ROMPE IL SONNO

Filippo di Monte
(*c.* 1521–1603)

42

* A (= B)

7. D'UN SI BEL FOCO

Giaches Wert
(1535–1596)

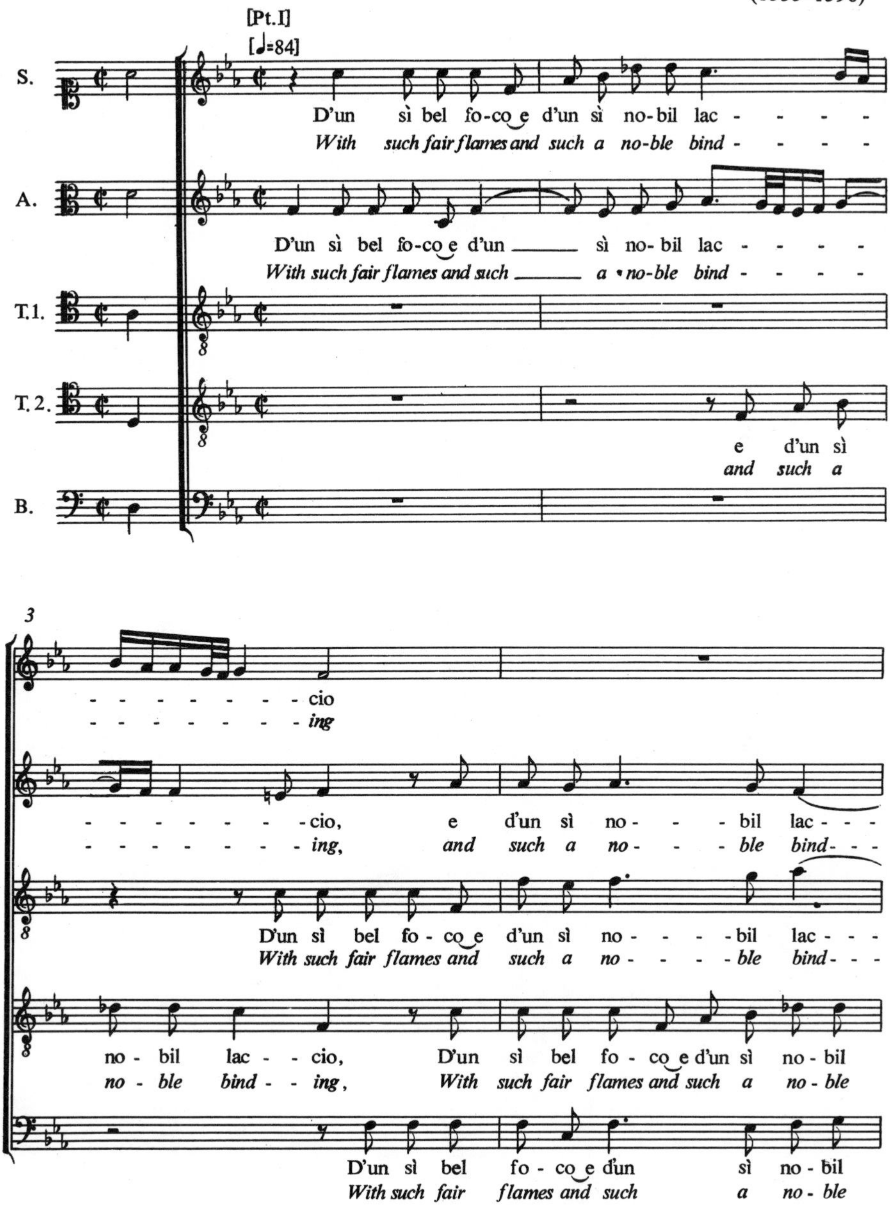

54

8. S'IO ESCA VIVO DE' DUBBIOSI SCOGLI

Orlandus Lassus
(*c.* 1532–1594)

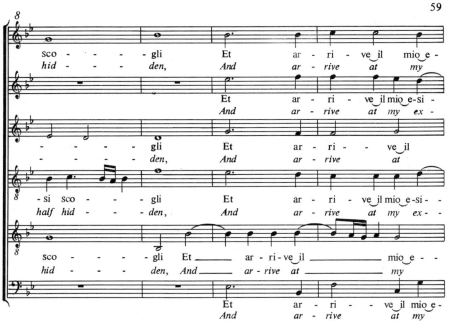

60

*) Octave lower.

*) Written out in full in the original, with S. I and II parts interchanged.

9. SONNO DILETTO E CARO

Andrea Gabrieli
(c. 1510–1586)

*) Repeat written out in full in the original, with both S. I and II and T. I and II interchanged.
The interchange should continue to the end.

10. LEGGIADRE NINFE

Luca Marenzio
(1553–1599)

74

*)These 2 bars consist of black minims and semibreves in all voices, descriptive of "ombroso valle."
Each bar is the same length as the previous bar.

Printed in England by WEST CENTRAL PRINTING CO. LTD., London and Suffolk.